CONTINUOUS IMPROVEMENT

CONTINUOUS IMPROVEMENT

Why it is Essential to the
Success of your Business
and How to Achieve It

Gregory J Kilbey

The term "continuous improvement" captures the idea that progress and success in business comes from attending to quality. In other words, forever looking for ways to do what we do better, more effectively and more efficiently. Continuous Improvement (CI) implies that we should never rest on our laurels, that our business and the environment in which we operate is continually changing, and that our on-going success is dependent upon how well we anticipate and adjust to change. Because the idea of CI is so appealing to visionary leaders committed to quality and excellence, many organisations try to implement CI programs. Unfortunately, most CI programs fail or, at best, achieve mediocre results. This book explores why this is so, and what can be done about it. Why are hopes not realized? Why is there resistance within the organisation from the outset or, perhaps more common, why does initial enthusiasm fade? Based on my experience working with all kinds of organisations implementing CI programs, I will explore with you the common reasons for failure and how you can avoid or address them. My belief and intention is that by reading this book, and carefully following the guidelines within it, you will be well on the way to introducing a sustainable CI program within your organisation and making CI an integral part of your corporate culture.

Contents

Introduction

A substantial amount of material has been written about Continuous Improvement (CI)—why we need it, how to do it, etc. Because there is so much information readily available, the way forward is more difficult than ever for many companies when trying to implement a sustainable continuous improvement program. This is partly due to the digital revolution and consequent disruption that has emerged as the 21st century began. This disruption has forced companies to pursue the digitisation as a way to streamline their core processes. Notwithstanding this, people and processes are still important to companies, no matter how much automation and associated digitization is achieved. Information bombardment and overload, enabled by the internet, has made it extremely difficult for managers and executives to implement a sustainable CI program.

The amount of information that is readily available, most of it confusing or contradictory, has clouded the landscape. This has led to inertia amongst leaders in how to proceed with a CI program that would benefit the organization immediately, and be sustainable, so it would survive the eventual turnover of the executive leadership.

For me, the driver to write this book has been the witnessing of a significant number of CI programs being launched in Australia and South-east Asia that had the best of intentions at the outset, failed at even the softest of measures of success, but that were salvaged to provide some perceived return on investment. Why is this happening? Well this book will look into some of the critical factors that have sent many a well-intentioned program down the path to failure. Equally importantly, I will show you a simple outline for a successful CI program, irrespective of the size or type of organization.

The book is written on the assumption that the reader will have, or is about to be involved in a CI program of some sort and has some background or level of understanding of this topic. I am cognizant of the immense amount of information that is readily available on this subject. My aim is to provide a way forward for the reader, an understanding of what typically can go wrong in implementing a CI program, and what actions can be undertaken to maximize its success.

The book will initially look at what's involved in a successful CI program, both from a structural viewpoint through to the type of outcomes that should be expected. I will also provide some context by introducing case studies of successful companies that have developed and maintained a successful CI program. Once I have established what a successful CI program should be, I will then critically analyse the mistakes that are often made by large companies when rolling out a CI program. There are a number of common factors that exist that need to be highlighted together with the consequences of these factors.

Finally, I will examine the building blocks for creating a successful program, the order in which the various activities are commenced and what needs to happen at both a 'grass-roots' level and at an executive level. I will provide an easy to follow structure that will provide the best chance at a successful implementation of a CI program.

The aim of this book is to provide a simple how-to guide in an easy to read style—with the use of jargon and academic concepts kept to a minimum. This book draws on personal experience that has been gained from over fifteen years in various CI programs. Some of this time has been spent as an internal change agent and also as an external consultant to various programs throughout Australia and South-East Asia.

Background

Continuous Improvement (CI) is nothing new to the corporate arena. Companies such as Toyota have been committed to CI for well over 60 years. CI can be expressed as "a culture of sustained improvement targeting the elimination of waste in all systems and processes of an organization"[1]. There are many other definitions of what CI is and they are all relevant. What needs to be clarified, however, is the difference between Process Improvement (PI) and CI. These terms are quite often used interchangeably and often in the wrong context. PI is not CI. PI is an organisational development concept in which a series of actions are taken by process owners to identify, analyse and improve existing business processes within an organization to increase profitability and/or performance often through reducing costs and accelerating process cycle time. Invariably PI is a *tactical* program involving a select number of people who are charged with this responsibility, whereas CI is a *strategic* program usually involving the entire workforce.

Toyota's CI program—known as Lean—is part of the Toyota Production System (TPS), which was created in the aftermath of World War 2. Since then, many different variations of CI have made their mark on the corporate world, all with different names. For example, TQM, Six Sigma, ITIL and Lean Six Sigma. I will say more about the similarities and differences between these programs below. My point here is that the large number of programs and variations on programs is itself an issue for businesses wanting to implement CI. Each decade seems to herald another version of CI for corporates to embrace en-masse with the assistance of nattily dressed consultants. The end result is virtually the same for many companies—a couple of early wins and not much else to show for the efforts that have been employed.

Armies of consultants are engaged to deliver what is initially promised as a panacea for all the issues that the company faces in terms of cost containment only to find that the results are far from what was expected. As a result, a flurry of finger pointing ensues that does nothing more than result in the departure of the sacrificial lamb and another re-organization of the company.

Although, as I have suggested, the plethora of CI programs and approaches is problematic for companies, there is a more important stumbling block to implementing a successful CI program. Surprisingly, the culprit is usually a lack of desire or willingness by senior management to make fundamental changes to the way that the company operates—i.e., to change its corporate culture.

According to corporate cultural change and CI consultant Philip Atkinson, "Organisations stand little chance of implementing Lean unless they have paid at least equal attention to creating the right culture, and the conditions and circumstances which can become the foundation for implementing change."[2] This I believe underpins the whole dilemma that confronts companies when a decision is made to introduce a CI program.

To some readers the terms such as 'Lean' and 'Six Sigma' may be confusing. Therefore, it's appropriate that I provide a brief explanation of the differences between Lean and Six Sigma, two of the best known approaches to CI. I will not go into significant detail as there is a plethora of books and articles already published that address these methodologies.

Lean, as I have mentioned, had its early origins as a methodology in post-war Japan as companies such as Toyota and Nissan built their car plants to take on the automotive industry in the late 1950s and 1960s. The term 'Lean' did not become part of the CI culture until it was coined by James Womack in the 1980s. The main focus of the Lean methodology is on the flow of a process to determine where bottlenecks exist and non-value adding steps occur in the process. The aim is to increase the velocity or speed of the process without having to employ additional resources.

Whilst Lean has been primarily a manufacturing methodology, it has been deployed successfully into service companies over the past 15-20 years to great success. One of the fundamental aspects of Lean is the systematic engagement of frontline workers, not just problem-solving teams or individuals within the business. Everyone has a role to remove waste from the way they work and to focus on continuous improvement.

Six Sigma's origins date back to the 1980s at Motorola. The term "Six Sigma" itself indicates its statistical origins. Six Sigma focuses on the quality of the product. Motorola, where the methodology was created in the 1980's had a quality issue with the communication products that were being produced. At the time, whilst sales were excellent, margins and customer satisfaction were being impacted by poor quality, which in turn caused unnecessary expense to repair defective products. 'Six Sigma' was coined by Bill Smith based on the quality scale that was created as the methodology was being developed. All processes were measured and given a sigma score which was calculated from the inherent variation in the process to business/customer specifications. As a result, a score of 'six sigma' indicates that the process will deliver less than 3.4 defective products in every million that are made. In other words, the process delivers defect-free product 99.9997% of the time. Since its development in Motorola, Six-Sigma has been deployed widely among Fortune 500 firms.

Since 2000, both these competing methodologies are often combined into one—Lean Six Sigma. The reason for this is that both methodologies work well in tandem in large companies, depending on whether the problem being solved is a quality or a process velocity issue. In recent times there has been an ongoing debate about whether it is better to concentrate on just Lean or Six Sigma or even incorporate execution methodologies such as Agile into the mix. However, I think these discussions are essentially avoiding the underlying issue. To put it another way, it is a bit like discussing the top speed of a car as part of the decision to purchase, when cars are not permitted to drive above 110 km/h on public roads and where every car being considered can easily travel at 110 km/h.

If implementing a successful CI program is so difficult, is it worth doing so?

Before discussing the characteristics of CI programs and how to successfully implement a sustainable program, it is important to get very clear about the benefits of doing so. Otherwise, why bother if the energy required is immense and the chances of failure are, statistically, high?

At the outset, I defined CI as a culture of improvement to eliminate system and process waste within an organization. However, we don't embark on a CI program just so that we can create this culture as the endgame. We embark on a CI program so that we can harvest the benefits of having this type of culture embedded in an organization.

There are of course financial benefits—reducing costs and/or increasing revenue—that flow from eliminating waste and other aspects of CI. Clearly, this is what drives the majority of executives to embark on a CI program. However, financial and other benefits can be short-term unless the underlying corporate culture supports CI. In my view, the greatest benefit of a CI program is cultural change, which enables an organisation to be flexible and nimble, continuously exploring and adapting to the ever-changing business environment.

There is an old saying, attributed to the Greek philosopher Heraclitus, that the only constant in life is change. This is true in the business world. The two case studies in the appendices of this book, General Electric and Toyota, are both companies that have prospered in an ever-changing business environment whilst many of their competitors have ceased to exist. Why is this? The answer is quite simple. In a robust CI culture, everyone is focused on why they are there in the first place—to serve the customer. When you have the customer at the centre of all your activities, then the focus is on delivering what the customer wants, in the most efficient manner. This will have the double effect of giving the customer what they want at the most competitive price.

When I first embarked on my CI journey some seventeen years ago, my mentor opened my eyes to this concept. He basically stated that if you are flexible in the way you deliver services at the lowest cost whilst providing what the customer wants, then you will have a distinct competitive advantage over your competitors. Competitors who don't have a CI program will no doubt have inherent waste in their processes. Therefore, to match price or service quality will be costly. The alternative is to surrender market share and/or profitability by not doing so.

The digitization of the world has created unique opportunities that in turn are signaling the end of long-established industries. Notwithstanding this, the companies that have a strong CI focus are well positioned to benefit the most from this significant change. These companies are able to adapt to the changing environment and seek out new opportunities. As an analogy to demonstrate this thinking, imagine a large double axle semi-trailer laden with containers (a large complex and inefficient company) and a single axle van (a nimble CI company). If both were driving down a road and had to make a sudden diversion to avoid an obstacle, the single axle van would have a better chance to avoid the obstacle given its better maneuverability. It is no different in the business world. History has shown many companies that were once dominant in their fields no longer exist, or have been taken over by rivals who have been better positioned to adapt to the changes in the marketplace.

What does a CI program look like?

CI practitioners do not always agree on the key aspects of a CI program. From my perspective, a proper CI program should have three main attributes: (1) Strategic Planning, (2) Process Improvement, and (3) Hygiene Behaviours— as illustrated below:

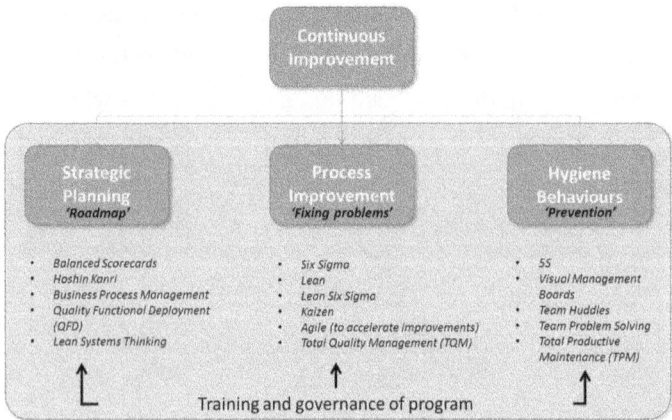

CI within some organisations only entails the second two aapects—Process Improvement and Hygiene Behaviours. This doesn't preclude these companies from extracting measurable benefits from their program. However, from my view, it doesn't constitute a complete CI program with the ultimate aim of becoming a cultural program and therefore sustainable.

Strategic Planning (The Roadmap)

I use the term "strategic planning" to refer to the overall strategic management of the program, which I also label as "the roadmap". From a strategic viewpoint there needs to be a sense of where the program is going and what it needs to achieve. When completing roadmaps, concepts such as "Balanced Scorecards", Hoshin Kanri, etc. are frequently used. (I discuss these concepts later in the book.) Such concepts assist a company strategically in creating the vision for the program and in turn how it relates to the overall corporate vision of the company. A good CI program should have a detailed 3-5 year strategic vision as well as formulated milestones to ensure that the organization is on track. In addition, there should be a tactical component which should have greater granularity over actions and measures of success for the next 12-18 months.

I have included Quality Functional Deployment (QFD) as a strategic lever and not as a process improvement methodology. QFD uses a highly structured process and matrix-based approach for product or process design, rather than improving a process. As such, its use is more strategic than tactical.

Process Improvement (Fixing problems)

Process improvement on its own is the 'firefighting approach' that companies often need when there is a process or product issue that is impacting revenue or costs. Often the issue impacts quality, cost, revenue or a combination of these factors. The problems invariably percolate up to senior management through feedback measurement loops, such as a decline in market share, uplift in customer complaints, or severe cost issues driven by product recalls, etc.

As a consequence, the need for CI is driven by a need to fix these large process-related problems as quickly as possible. In other words, putting out any fires that are adversely impacting operations or profitability within the company. Companies often use other terms for these actions—Business Re-engineering, Business Transformation, Process Excellence, Business Centre of Excellence, etc.

Just implementing process improvement is not CI as all it's doing is fixing the problems as they occur—not preventing them. Like most fires, when you walk away, they have a habit of re-igniting in the same place or somewhere else, which then requires the same activity to occur to remove the problem.

Hygiene Behaviours (Prevention)

Hygiene behaviours or factors are the disciplines that usually underpin a CI program. I call them preventative methods, because these actions are usually undertaken to ensure that issues are resolved as soon as they are recognised and the workplace environment does not contribute to inefficiency. These preventative measures can be classed into two different buckets: (1) housekeeping activities, and (2) localized problem solving.

Methods such as 5S, VMBs and Team Huddles apply to the way a business operates and as such are really housekeeping measures. 5S (Sort, Set in Order, Shine, Standardize, Sustain) at its core describes how to organise a work space (this can either be the shop floor, factory or corporate office space) for efficiency and effectiveness by identifying and storing the items used, maintaining the area and items, determining optimal layouts and sustaining this environment. VMBs or Visual Management Boards are simple displays of information and are key communication tools in a lean environment whose intention is to provide information at a glance. There are several different types of visual management boards, including boards for continuous improvement, project status, and operational status.

Localized problem solving, which include: Team Problem Solving and Total Productive Maintenance (TPM) is about empowering the workforce to solve their own problem rather than calling upon someone or another team to solve it for them. It is about ensuring that the small problems can be effectively solved at a local level before they manifest themselves into greater issues that need to be solved in a process improvement environment.

What does success in CI look like?

'Success' is one of those terms that is used too frequently to form a judgment on the activities of individuals or companies. Too often we forget that success is a noun used to generically describe the outcome. The dictionary meaning of 'success' is the accomplishment of an aim or purpose. So, when we talk about success, we need to be mindful that the outcome is predicated by whatever was agreed to as criteria for success at the beginning. From a generic perspective, a successful CI program should be able to (if we use our definition from before) create a culture of sustained improvement targeting the elimination of waste in all systems and processes of an organization.

If this is the case, we need to focus on culture. But what does this mean? Understanding an organisation's culture is difficult enough. Changing that culture is even more challenging. CEOs often make public statements to the effect that we need to change the culture of our company. Unfortunately, a culture change is unable to be achieved in a short timeframe. Executives, however, typically judge the success or otherwise over 6 to 12 months. This situation creates a disconnect between what's achievable and what's expected.

A successful CI program, if we look at the examples from history to date, is something that has taken time to create and has had many challenges. At its simplest, a successful CI program should involve everyone from the CEO down to the shop floor. It should form part of the DNA of the company and involve everyone including new starters from day one as they are inducted into the company. The effectiveness of the program management is measured by the way that it drives the company to improve the way it works and the way the people work.

Companies that have managed to create a successful CI program usually have the following traits:

1. A robust measurement system to measure not only the benefits in terms of money saved through efficiencies, but also the effect it has on customer satisfaction.

2. A CI learning program that has a clearly defined pathway that ensures leaders within the company have a certain level of expertise in CI.

3. An organisation-wide understanding that everyone is responsible for CI, not just a department with a select number of people trained to 'fix issues'.

Whilst these traits don't seem too onerous to have in place to ensure the success of a CI program, experience suggests that fully implementing these traits is extremely challenging.

What is BPM and is it a substitute for CI?

I have found some degree of confusion in regards to the difference between Business Process Management (BPM) and CI. Some people believe the two terms are interchangeable. However, this is not the case, and the distinction is important.

BPM is widely used because it can be effective in times of crisis. According to the Association for Information and Image Management (AIIM), BPM is "a way of looking at and then controlling the processes that are present in an organization. It is an effective methodology to use in times of crisis to make certain that the processes are efficient and effective, as this will result in a better and more cost efficient organization."[3]

A survey was recently conducted by the University of Western Sydney (UWS) in which a majority of the respondents indicated that their understanding of BPM was "a top-down methodology designed to organize, manage and measure the organization based on the organisation's core processes."[4]

Given either of these definitions, it is evident that BPM requires a shift in the strategic thinking of a company. Traditional companies have driven the business through departments that are organized across the whole value chain (i.e., silos), whereas BPM requires a cultural shift for the company to rethink the business in terms of enterprise-wide process models that are the key drivers to the business. The process models are then broken down into core, management or support processes and process owners are attributable to each process. In previous roles, I have been part of the ongoing war within these traditional companies where the sales team blames the back office, the back office blames the sales office, and so on. The aim of BPM is to align everyone to the customer and ensure that there is only one person responsible for the process (i.e., the Process Owner).

BPM is far more than just identifying and aligning business processes. The first step to implement a BPM culture is to understand where the business is currently at. This requires an audit of each business unit to determine the maturity of the business in managing its processes. These audits are conducted in line with a recognized BPM framework— such as American Society for Quality (ASQ), Australian Business Excellence Framework (ABEF) or European Foundation for Quality Management (EFQM). The aim of the audit is simply to assess the maturity of the business in terms of both managing its processes and improving them.

From this starting point, the focus of BPM is to shift the maturity of the company towards 'world's best practice'.

You will no doubt recognize that there are a number of similarities between BPM and CI. The main difference is that BPM is an overarching framework which in turn utilizes CI to improve the business. BPM is not a CI program and companies that use BPM will need some type of mechanism to address processes that are not being adequately managed. Consequently, a number of companies have made the strategic decision to adopt CI as part of their BPM framework. Conversely, whilst there will be benefits to achieve if only a CI program is adopted, these benefits can be significantly uplifted if a BPM program is also deployed. One of the main benefits is having an overarching strategic and holistic view of the business from a process perspective. This in turn can achieve a more targeted CI program—knowing which parts of the business need the immediate focus and also eliminating duplicated CI activities from occurring.

What is customer centricity?

The phrase 'Customer Centric' has been receiving a significant amount of airtime among executives and senior managers at major corporations in the past 3-5 years. At one place, where I was engaged in some CI work, the standard joke among senior managers was to always ensure that the term 'customer centric' was mentioned at least a couple of times in any business case that was going up to steering committees for approval. In effect, it was just a 'buzz word' that was used without anyone really understanding what the actual meaning was.

Even as recently as my last consulting engagement, this term has become part of the strategy of the company. When I asked a couple of managers that I was working with what that term meant to them, there was a distinct difficulty in articulating in simple language what their customer centric strategy was. However, when you look at any definition of what it means, you soon realize that any company in business should be having customer centricity as their core strategy. Customer centricity is simply defined as creating a positive customer experience at either the point of sale or post sale. Retail and service businesses survive or fail based on this simple premise. Net Promoter Score (NPS) is a metric that is usually employed to gauge whether a company is achieving this or not.

One of the main reasons for adopting a CI program should be to improve the customer centricity of an organization. When you remember that Lean is about increasing the speed of processes and Six Sigma about improving the quality of products, this is why we are doing this in the first place, to make the process more responsive in delivering what the customer wants. The successful application of either or both of these methodologies should be creating a better experience for the customer. Some of the companies that I have worked for in the past 10-15 years have even adopted this as a mission statement, using terms such as "Customer driven Lean Six Sigma" and "Six Sigma Customer Experience" to describe their programs.

Linking CI programs to BPM and Customer Centric Activities

In recent times, there has been much activity in the Business Process Management (BPM) space among executives. The issue that comes up frequently with the competing priorities of BPM and CI, is determining whether one is more important than the other or which one should I focus on first? Unfortunately, for both of these questions there is no easy answer. Both BPM and CI are important to companies. The good news is that they are designed to co-exist and should exist together in a proper CI framework.

During the 1990s, when Six Sigma was gaining traction around a majority of the Fortune 500 companies, BPM had its genesis. Its initial focus was IT based with an aim to automate business processes. However, this concept was extended to workflow management systems and processes involving human interventions. The similarities to Six Sigma and Lean are quite evident in the tools that are employed in rolling out BPM. Tools such as RACI charts, SIPOCs and process mapping are widely used in CI and BPM toolkits.

More recently, BPM's focus has been on compliance with the ever increasing need of companies to comply with government regulations and company policies. From my experience, the concept appeals to a significant number of COOs. However, again as with CI, the will and motivation to properly implement BPM is found wanting. The need to map the company processes and set up a BPM framework usually taxes the enthusiasm of many a COO, which results more often than not in the BPM program being abandoned at the next corporate restructure.

Why do CI programs to fail?

This is a question that is often asked of me and others at the many conferences I have attended as either a speaker or attendee. Unfortunately, the answer is not easy to package up in a one or two minute response. At face value, given the benefits of conducting a CI program and what is involved, it is inconceivable that there could be so many failures. However, this is unfortunately the reality and as such we need to investigate why this is the case. Too often, companies will not learn from the mistakes of those who have gone before, only to suffer the same fate.

Therefore, before embarking on the deployment of a CI program, the causes of failure or a sub-optimal result should be investigated so that we can learn from these experiences. From my involvement in various CI programs from Six Sigma to Lean to Lean Six Sigma deployments at large companies, I have experienced attempts that commenced with the best of intentions only to limp to either a painful death or a result similar to a coma. The first point that I want to stress is that it has nothing to do with whether Lean is better than Six Sigma or vice versa;

both are excellent methodologies. When implemented properly, both can deliver an improvement to the bottom line of between 5-10% of net profit after tax (NPAT). The problems are invariably associated with the deployment of the program within the company.

In summary, the common causes of the failure of a CI program can be attributed to one or more of the following factors:

I.   The program is not driven or championed by the CEO.

II. Unrealistic short-term expectations of the program at the outset (overpromise and under-deliver).

III. The program does not involve everyone in the company. A select number of people have been given the honour of being CI focused.

IV. The CI program is not linked to the business strategy.

V.   Balanced scorecards and Key Performance Indicators (KPIs) do not reflect the investment in CI.

A number of these factors will already resonate with readers, particularly if they have been involved in a corporate-wide initiative that was launched to much fanfare only to soon disappear from the consciousness of all employees.

The cause of program failure can be attributed to all or some of these reasons when conducting a post-mortem. However, to be honest, some of these factors are a consequence of another. This will become apparent as we dissect each of these factors.

I. The program is not driven or championed by the CEO.

If I was asked to name the one overarching root cause as to why CI programs ultimately fail, this would be my main candidate.

A strategy is owned by the Board. This strategy is put to the Board for approval by the CEO. In a less overt way, the CEO is responsible for setting the culture of an organization. As a result, every employee in the company looks to the CEO for direction as would any soldier look to their commanding officer in warfare. Therefore, whatever is important to the CEO is important to the employee. I have personally viewed examples where a CEO has put in place a CI program and championed the program to great success only for it to falter when the CEO departs after one or two years. Quite often, one of the first casualties when a new CEO arrives is the pet initiative of the previous CEO.

Ten years ago, I was a Transformation Lead at a large telecommunications company in Australia. This company had launched a Six Sigma program 3 years earlier and had achieved significant success during that time. Over

5,000 people had received some CI training in Six Sigma techniques and the company realized benefits in excess of $300 million. In addition, when a question was included in the employee engagement survey to determine the level of awareness around the Six Sigma program, the last reported score was close to 60%. Given all these factors, this was as close to a successful deployment as any that has been witnessed in Australia. Within the following 2 years, the program was in tatters. Most of the key resources had either departed the company voluntarily or involuntarily and customer service measures had deteriorated rapidly. What was the cause of this sudden and dramatic decline? A change in CEO. The previous CEO who had been at the helm of the company for some 8 years did not have his contract renewed by the Board, which decided to take a different direction. In retrospect, some members of the Board may have regretted that decision.

There is a common saying that it takes 5-8 years to change the culture of a company. If that is the case, this example provided some insight as to why this is the case. The program was in its third year and had not been fully embedded; the culture had not been fully transformed into a CI culture. Consequently, a change in the company's strategic direction resulted in this outcome. Of course, it could be argued, if it was the 5th, 8th or 10th year, there is no guarantee that a CI culture could have been sustained.

To counter that argument, the often quoted example of General Electric (GE) comes to mind. Jack Welch popularized Six Sigma during the 1990s. He was the leading advocate of Six Sigma during his tenure and oversaw the transformation of GE into a dynamic multinational behemoth. Six Sigma in GE was truly entrenched as the CI program with the program embedded in the way people worked and also as part of the corporate structure. There was no way to become a senior executive at GE without being a trained and certified Six Sigma Black Belt. Following Jack Welch's inevitable retirement after many years as CEO, the company today, still embraces a CI culture with the addition of Lean Principles to their CI toolkit.

II. Unrealistic short-term expectations of the program at the outset (overpromise and under-deliver)

Another way to get a CI program off to a wrong start is to launch with much fanfare and provide expectations that don't match the investment being made. A common mistake that's made is when a company sends its senior executives on a 'study tour' to witness CI companies and how they operate. This is not in itself an issue. In fact, I strongly advocate some type of investigation and benchmarking before undertaking a CI program. The problem is that these executives commonly make the mistake of touring these companies through a prism of today's culture of 'immediacy' and not understanding that they are witnessing the end result of many years of trial-and-error and solid commitment across the entire company. As a consequence, the executives return to their business with the best of intentions, but with a mistaken belief that they can implement an 'off the shelf' CI solution in a 12 to 18 month timeframe.

This is commonly known as the 'iceberg principle'. We see the tip of the iceberg (what is visible) and believe that's all that there is to it. We witness someone at the top of their sport or endeavor, see their performance is effortless, and imagine we can easily replicate the same result. At the end of every Olympic Games, some of the key glamour sports always brace for the 'Olympic effect', where many people take up a sport after witnessing it on television, only to abandon it sometime later when they realize that the mastery of the skills requires more effort and motivation than what they're willing to give.

If you queried any transformation consultant who has experience in developing CI programs, the response would be that the best result would be a break-even result by Year 2. That is, a recoupment of costs (including start-up costs) by the benefits achieved from the program to that point in time. Any outcome beyond a break-even result should be considered an exception. The first 2 years is all about setting up frameworks and governance, in addition to training existing staff or recruiting trained professionals into the business.

III. The program does not involve everyone in the company. A select number of people have been given the honour of being CI focussed.

In the early stages of a CI program, a select number of people are usually trained to get the program going. However, it should be part of the overarching strategy to roll out some degree of CI training to all people in the company within a 5 year timeframe.

When I was first trained as a Six Sigma Black Belt, I had to apply for the role and go through a rigorous selection process. The aim of this process was to ensure that the company selected the 'best of the best', so to speak. Whilst this was an excellent strategy, as it built a desire among employees to be one of the select few, it did nothing for the long term CI endeavours of the company. In fact, within 2 years, it became apparent that the resources had become constrained because all the Black Belt's time was consumed in solving business problems, but not improving the business long term. Furthermore, the heads of business units became disillusioned about the program, as these very business units were competing for the resources of a small number of Black Belts to solve their problems. Hence their enthusiasm for the program began to wane.

IV. The CI program is not linked to the business strategy.

This may seem a strange reason for failure. CI programs should be self-serving and consequently not needed to be linked to the strategy. In other words, if we are continuously improving the business why do we need a direct linkage to the strategy?

Unfortunately, no matter how altruistic or logical something may seem, it does not guarantee success. Organizations and companies today attempt to have in place what are called 'balanced scorecards', which were originated by Dr Robert Kaplan. Balanced scorecards align business activities to the vision, strategy and goals of the organization. Typically, there are four components or perspectives on the scorecard—financial, customer, process and learning/growth goals. This is important, because balance is important to sustainability, and anything that's not covered by the balanced scorecard will fall outside the focus of the business. There is a common saying that 'people only care about what they get measured on' and because of this, if the CI program is not part of the business strategy, and in turn is not being measured, there is little chance that employees and managers are going to devote much energy to it.

V. Balanced scorecards and Key Performance Indicators (KPIs) do not reflect the investment in CI

As I mentioned in the previous section, balanced scorecards are the drivers of business strategy. So, if there is to be an investment in CI, the investment must form part of the strategy and be reflected in the balance scorecards.

This was evident when I coached CI project managers (Black Belts) who had been working on 'critical projects' and had experienced sponsor issues such as cancellation of meetings or not making resources available to assist with the progress of the project. After finally meeting with the sponsor who was usually an executive, I discovered that it wasn't that important to them, as it was not reflected in their scorecards/KPIs. They have had all the best intentions from the outset, but when other issues got in the way such as deadlines for key projects or initiatives that were directly related to the scorecard, the project was pushed to the side.

This also goes for part-time CI project managers. A common occurrence in Lean Six Sigma rollouts over the past 10 years has been to have part-time 'green belts' taking on projects. This in theory is an excellent idea as the aim is to build the capability of people within the organization to solve process-related problems. However, unless their involvement in doing this project is reflected in their KPIs, the delivery of the project will inevitably be delayed and most likely not completed at all. As a program manager, I have had too many discussions around the slow execution of projects with a senior executive responsible for the deployment within the company where the root cause of the issue was no allowance for the projects in the KPIs of the individuals.

CI versus Offshoring:
the 21st century dilemma

The current proliferation of offshoring programs among well established companies raises important questions for CI programs: (1) Is offshoring a better value proposition for a company in comparison to a robust CI program, and (2) can both offshoring and CI co-exist within a company?

Around the early part of this century, in tandem with the acceleration of the digital revolution, the concept of transferring your back office functions to where you could exploit a lower wage cost gained serious momentum. Many companies explored and moved significant back office functions to low wage precincts such as Bangalore. The main driver for this was the cost arbitrage that this function transfer delivered. I was at a major Australia bank during this time and the cost arbitrage was almost 6:1. When the business case to transfer these functions to Bangalore was approved, the average salary of a payments clerk in Australia was around A$70,000 versus a salary in Bangalore of around A$12,000. The original business case at the time was pitched at an employee cost saving of around \$12-14 million per annum for that department alone. However, the actual benefit in the first 2 years was significantly less than this business case estimate. Why? Well there were 2 distinct problems that were not forseen at the time the business case was completed, but should have been, if basic economics and operational planning had been considered.

This first issue was the evaporation of the cost arbitrage due to market dynamics. First year economics students could have advised that if there are competing demands for a supply then the cost of the supply will increase. As was the case with offshoring to Bangalore, a number of companies from all over the world started offshoring and as a result, the supply of educated university graduates was challenged by companies needing staff to fill their back office centres. The consequence of this was large staff turnovers or alternatively increasing salaries to reduce the turnover rates and retain talented staff.

Within 18 months the average salary in the Bangalore centre had increased from around \$12,000 to \$18,000/\$20,000. This did not take into account the high recruitment costs that were coupled to a staff turnover rate of 20%.

The second issue with moving a function to another jurisdiction was the creation of political and market risk. Early on in the offshoring program, when the initial payment functions were moved to Bangalore, the issue of market risk became apparent when a city-wide strike was called in Bangalore and the payment functions were not staffed. Given that the original on-shore payment teams had been made redundant, this created issues that had to be overcome. Consequently, skeleton onshore teams were put in place to cover this situation and also operated as an overflow and as a service quality team. The issue of quality also became a problem, because the quality of work in Bangalore was not of the same standard as the original teams that were offshored. This was not surprising given the large turnover of staff in the Bangalore office and the training of staff was probably not of a sufficient standard. As a consequence, the cost of creating onshore teams that exist as a 'quality assurance function' had not been foreseen and were not accounted for in the original business case.

Offshoring from a CI perspective creates significant challenges. Not the least is the hand-off to another time-zone which can create significant delays in a process. Coupled with this, is the addition of checking functions which adds further time delays into processes. I witnessed this very issue when these functions were offshored to Bangalore. As a case in point, one of the functions that was offshored was a bank statement reprint process. Prior to the offshoring of the function, 95% of statements were issued to customers within 3 days. Following the transfer of this function to Bangalore, this metric reduced to less than 50% being processed within 3 days due to the 5-hour time delay between the two offices. This delay forced actions that could have been completed same day moving into the next day, and requests sitting in queues waiting to be actioned. In summary, whilst the business may have reduced their back office costs, the cost to customer service was negatively impacted.

You can probably guess from my narrative that I'm not a fan of offshoring functions to lower cost environments. My view is based on the fact that a majority of these decisions are often based on a false economy. Decisions are based on cost differentials that could change within a 1 to 2 year time frame, which can significantly erode the benefits that were envisaged at the outset. Furthermore, from a process perspective, which is my area of interest, offshoring does nothing to improve a process. The process of offshoring introduces significant hand-offs which create delays and quality issues that need to be addressed. However, the decision to off-shore will not be going away in the immediate future. Particularly as the fixation on short term fixes to long term business structural problems continues to exist. It is far easier for companies to just move inefficient processes to a lower cost jurisdiction than to fundamentally improve the processes.

How to create a successful CI program?

Once we understand the root causes of failure, only then are we in a position to prescribe the solution to the problem. Given the factors previously highlighted that contribute to failed CI programs, I have detailed the following remedies that will assist in the successful deployment of a CI program. It is not whether Lean, Six Sigma, Lean Six Sigma or Quality Circles, etc. as an underlying methodology has been utilized, as these have all be proven to work. It is how these programs are deployed into an organisation that will determine their success or failure.

This brings to mind an old saying: 'a carpenter should never blame his tools for poor workmanship'. The same is applicable here. We should not blame the methodology for the failure of the program, but the way it is deployed.

Senior executives need to understand that culture change is required

Once it has been agreed that a CI program is to be rolled out in an organization, the senior executives across the company need to be not only trained in what they need to know from an executive viewpoint, they must also change the way they work.

Culture change to align to the CI program is an integral part of its success. This is not a short term initiative that will be achieved in a 6-12 month timeframe. In reality, successful culture change is a 5 to 7 year journey. The change begins with the executives developing clear messaging about what it means for the company and the length of time it will take for the company to achieve this. Coupled with this, a decisive change in behaviours is required at the outset, so that executives are seen to be not only 'talking the talk' but also 'walking the walk'. In my experience, employees are quick to ascertain whether a company is serious about a corporate-wide initiative. If there is a perception that the senior management is not totally on-board, then acceptance on the shop-floor will be difficult to achieve.

Alignment of CI program to corporate strategy

As I stated earlier, the corporate strategy is a company's roadmap that has been set by the CEO and board. As such, all business units within the company should be aligning their business strategy to the overarching corporate strategy. This is no different with the CI program. The CI program must be either a part of the corporate strategy or be aligned to it.

I will give an example to show why this is important. Several years ago, I was working at a public listed company associated with the mining industry in Australia. Lean Six Sigma was introduced with much initial fanfare. However, following its launch it lost significant momentum as the program was sold on the basis of making the company more efficient and reducing *costs*. This in isolation sounded like a fair proposition for any publicly listed company. However, at the time, the strategy for the company was aligned to *revenue* growth as were the corresponding KPIs. In tandem with the mining boom at the time, the company was entirely focused on building its revenue base. As a result, there was virtually no buy-in to Lean Six Sigma by the senior management and it struggled significantly to gain any foothold as a corporate CI program. Within a couple of years the program was no more than a small department that was utilised to look at cost reduction initiatives such as supply chain cost or working capital (tactical responses) rather than a cultural mindset where everyone was involved.

This simply illustrates how a program needs to be aligned to the corporate strategy, particularly across business unit strategy and KPIs As an experienced Lean Six Sigma consultant, when I coach project managers, the first advice I offer as they embark on their process improvement project is to identify the KPIs of the process owner and the people within the process. A mismatch of KPIs is usually one of the key causes for process failure. There is an old adage that was taught to me over 15 years ago by my original Master Black Belt coach: "Values drives Behaviours." That simple statement is the most powerful lesson that anyone can learn in life about human behavior.

What a person values will largely determine how they act and behave. People in organisations understandably value what is measured. So, if you have a quality problem in a process and the people in the process are being measured on productivity and throughput only, then your problem lies in the way that you are measuring performance. It is not a question of people not caring about quality, but when they are under pressure, they know that they are being measured on throughput and productivity, so quality will be the first casualty in this process.

Long-term commitment with CEO endorsement highly visible

I touched on this briefly earlier when discussing the be-haviours of senior executives. One of the key aspects of any successful program is the long term commitment by executives, in particular the CEO. Coupled with this, careful messaging needs to ensure there is no ambiguity or perception that the CI program is just a quick fix or the 'program of the moment'.

I have now been through two relatively successful CI programs that were completely dismantled as a result of a change in CEO. In addition, I have worked at three companies where the CI program never got off the ground as a result of the CEO not being on-board. What I mean by being on-board is not tacit compliance. One of the failed CI programs that I was involved with, supposedly had the support of the CEO, however, not one communication went out from his office promoting or advising the staff of the importance of the program. Support in executive meetings and provision of a CI budget does not constitute endorsement of a program.

Long term commitment needs to involve careful messaging that a successful CI program will take years not months to implement and will involve cultural change across the entire company. It will also mean that in some cases, a return on investment may not be apparent until the second or third year of its operation, depending on the speed and depth of the rollout.

Operational Performance to be visible through quality metrics

"You can only manage what you measure"; "In God we trust, everyone else bring me data." These and countless other quotes I have used in the training room and also often heard in presentations are usually attributed to people like

Edwards Deming—the pioneer and leading light of total quality management (TQM). The underlying emphasis of these statements is around the need for data to manage operational performance. Furthermore, the metrics that we use to measure operational performance need to be representative of the business that we are managing. Too often, metrics become a casualty of convenience. As an example, in a previous role I was asked to create business dashboards which were to include metrics that were aligned to balanced scorecards. Where there were gaps or misalignment in the metrics, the common reasons provided were comments such as "that has been the way that we have always measured performance" or "our systems can only provide these measures". Performance measurement is critical to success and therefore measurements need to be accurate. If systems need to be changed to deliver accurate reporting, then so be it. The return on the cost of these changes will be substantial when you consider that effective CI programs can deliver millions of dollars in benefits both from improved processes and changed behaviours.

What are the key measures of success for a CI program?

As I mentioned at the outset, success has to be clearly defined before the key measures of success can be discussed and agreed upon. Too often, CI deployments are reduced to just metrics around the numbers trained in CI, and projects completed (good, bad or indifferent). Therefore, if we use the definition of success that was presented earlier—a culture of sustained improvement targeting the elimination of waste in all systems and processes of an organization—then success should be directly aligned with measures of improvement and the elimination of waste.

Consequently, there are a number of key measures for the success of a CI program:

i.   The CI program is measured in actual $ benefits (hard benefits vs soft benefits).

ii. The right people are trained and there is a follow-on after the initial project and certification.

iii. There is an overall cultural metric employed that is measured in conjunction with annual employee surveys.

iv. CI is aligned to Learning and Development (L&D) pathways to promote and continue the culture change.

i. The CI program is measured in actual $ benefits (hard vs soft benefits)

Whilst this is an obvious measure, it is often the first measure to be jettisoned in a CI program that has not been established correctly or not aligned to the company's key strategic goals. I have made reference to the hard versus soft benefits for an important reason. These terms of 'hard' or 'soft' when measuring benefits are quite common in transformation and CI programs. A hard benefit is defined as a saving that can be attributed to a general ledger code in the balance sheet and, as such, there should be no ambiguity about the saving in dollars that are reported. An example of this could be a reduction in 'write-offs' or 'bad and doubtful debts'. These are actual general ledger accounts so if a program of work or a project was success-ful in reducing either of these, this could be reported as a hard benefit.

Conversely, a soft benefit is where it is difficult to attribute the savings to a general ledger account. This could be due to the way the project was established in the first instance or through poor reporting attributes. An example of this could be a productivity saving (a common method used in many companies for expressing CI benefits). A project could be delivered with a productivity saving of say 10,000 employee hours per annum. The problem with this is that we can't say with any conviction that this saving has flowed through to a general ledger account in a measurable way, such as employee costs.

This type of reporting of soft benefits can be expressed in $ terms and then used in intra-company reporting of the program benefits. The danger in this type of reporting is that it can give a false impression of the true success or failure of a program. It can also undermine the success of a program where people express little faith in the figures that are quoted. I have often heard the comment "they weren't real benefits" used in leadership meetings when referring to the dollar benefits of a project or program. Another soft benefit is around 'cost avoidance'. Many risk projects can attribute a cost avoidance figure expressed in dollars that may seem sensational, but under further scrutiny, the dollar amount represents an estimate of likely loss at an upper end estimate of a 1 in 100,000 scenario.

Whilst I am not against the claiming of productivity hours, cost avoidance, revenue uplift (if you can't isolate revenue increase that was directly attributable to the project) etc., I do have an issue when these savings are expressed in dollar terms and then included in reporting to 'dress up' the success of a program. The long term success of a CI program should be based in actual hard benefits so that there is no ambiguity as to what the program means in bottom line benefits. Yes, the reporting can include other benefits such as customer satisfaction, risk avoidance, etc., but these types of benefits should not be a main driver in companies where the main focus is in increasing revenue and reducing costs.

As a final point on this matter, when a company focuses on hard benefits as a true measure of success of the program, project selection is the main beneficiary. I have seen too many poorly defined project charters where there appears to be no measurable hard benefit. When this has been queried, I have received numerous replies from the project manager and sponsor that the project is important to the business. I find this difficult to reconcile in a proper CI environment. If the project is important to the business but we are unable to measure it in hard benefits, then I can only assume project scoping has not been executed correctly. This means that the culprit is either a poorly defined project statement of work or the measures of success for the project have not been properly defined.

ii. The right people are trained and there is a follow-on after the initial project and certification

What do I mean by the right people? Well, definitely someone who wants to be trained and be an advocate for

CI. This may seem to be an obvious statement, but all too often I have seen poor performing employees nominated for CI roles as a way to exit them from front line or operational roles. A CI program should not be a dumping ground for average or poor performing employees. People with a strong desire to challenge the status quo or fix problems should be encouraged into these roles. People who are passionate about CI will be leading advocates in any business.

Once the identified persons are trained, there should be a clearly defined role for them in the business, which should include an initial training project and follow-on work that should lead to a recognized certification (e.g. Green Belt, Black Belt, Sensai Master, etc.)

In addition, managers should not be exempt from the CI program; their training should be in tandem with the training of their identified resources. Their understanding of what CI is to the business is critical to the success of the rollout of CI. I have seen well trained and passionate CI resources wasted by a manager unable to effectively utilize this resource in the business through lack of training themselves, and indifference to the CI program.

The training of CI resources is a two-way street. The business is spending time and money training the resource, which in return is assisting in transforming the business through CI. In effect, this should translate into bottom line benefits to the business and a better, more committed workforce.

One of the complaints or issues raised when discussing the calibre of candidates for training in CI is their marketability in the greater workforce with these skills and perhaps becoming a 'flight risk'. I find this comment or argument quite concerning, as it gives an alarming insight as to the way that some companies nurture their talent. If HR managers or business leaders truly believe that this is an issue then to me it leads to the belief that these people are either underpaying their workforce (not valuing them appropriately) or have not properly thought out succession planning in a business. The training of valuable staff, or staff who are passionate about CI, is an important part of ensuring that the business can create better succession planning and also limit staff turnover. When trained CI resources have left an organization, the main driver behind their decision has often not has been monetary (which may seem surprising), but because their recently obtained skillset has not been valued by the organization or by their manager in terms of promotion or career pathing.

iii. There is an overall cultural metric employed that is measured in conjunction with annual employee surveys

For CI to become part of the culture of a company, a long term view is required, remembering that it will take at least

5-7 years to adequately embed this cultural shift. To determine the success of the cultural change, a suitable measure needs to be implemented and tracked to ensure that the change is successful.

The challenge is to find a suitable measure to gauge this shift in the company's culture. This is not an easy or clearcut task and from my experience there is no fool-proof measure. Some of the measures that I have seen employed focus on the awareness aspects of the CI program through an annual engagement survey. That is, the question could be phrased along the lines:"Are you aware that we have a CI program at X?" Additional questions could be: "Are you regularly updated as to the progress of the CI program?" and "Have you been offered an opportunity to be trained as part of the CI program?" The responses to these questions will provide valuable insight as to the cultural awareness of the program across the entire company and can also indicate where there are 'black spots'—i.e. low engagement scores. This type of diagnostic is important to ensure that there are no constraints to an organisation-wide deployment

Including these types of questions in corporate wide employee engagement surveys provides useful data easily. Firstly, because the sample size is considerable, there should be a minimization of sample bias. Secondly, incorporating such questions as part of the annual employee engagement survey does not create a further impost upon the employees or the people charged with conducting the surveys.

To date, I have seen CI and cultural surveys being incorporated into employee engagement surveys in two organisations effectively. This is a perfect place to gather information about a CI program and measure, on a year-on-year basis, its cultural effectiveness.

iv. CI is aligned to Learning & Development (L&D) pathways to promote and continue the cultural change

In my experience, a lack of Human Resource (HR) involvement in CI programs is common. This certainly does not assist with the long term cultural change that's needed to embed a successful CI program. Given the supreme importance of cultural change as a key ingredient to a successful CI program, lack of HR involvement is a problem. HR is not only responsible for recruitment and management of staff, but also Learning & Development (L&D). L&D is a vital component when you consider that cultural change involves training people to do things differently.

My experience at one of these deployments appears to hold the key to this problem. At that time, I asked the program manager why there was no HR representation on the program steering committee. The answer to this question was a statement to the effect that HR don't feel that there's any need for them to be involved in the program. Conse-quently, no HR people were trained in CI, nor was there any uptake or interest in being involved. At this particular company, I noted with some amusement that HR were at pains to defend their woeful recruitment process, which forced managers to take up to 6 months to recruit people externally. Not only did this affect productivity, it was challenging for the company to attract the right people. It would appear that there was a desperate need for their involvement in the Lean Six Sigma program.

So why the lack of engagement? This is not a question that is easily answered. In some of the deployments that I've been involved with, the CI program was considered an operational issue to improve customer processes. As such, the HR departments in those companies had a misguided belief that there was no need for them to be involved other than in their usual role of assisting in recruitment. This lack of engagement could be due solely to the fact that the program manager didn't effectively engage HR with the benefits of being involved in such a program.

In reflection, I think HR's lack of engagement was also due to not aligning their skills to the program itself. At the de-ployment I mentioned previously, there was no alignment of the CI training being conducted with the L&D depart-ment, so it was probably more of "if you don't need us, we don't need you." At one of my more recent engagements, where I was responsible for the training of staff in CI, I worked closely with the HR function there, in particular the L&D department. This in turn proved to be an invaluable experience. The L&D team introduced me to learning pathways and how to re-frame the training along these lines. The more HR learned what we were trying to do, the more they became involved. In the end we were invited to work with them on a number of their core processes, such as, payroll, recruitment and onboarding. Improving these processes not only produced significant bottom line benefits but received positive exposure about the improvement in HR functions.

Aligning CI to L&D pathways taught me something that is often overlooked when implementing a CI framework. The importance is two-fold. Firstly, L&D control the training function and manage mandatory training modules such as workplace safety. In addition, L&D create the recommended training pathways for various roles within the organization. It was through this mechanism that I was able to have an online mandatory CI training included as part of the requirements of all roles within a particular area. The second importance is that it allows for CI training to be part of the career management process. This is important if we are looking to embed the program in the company as part of its DNA.

Embedding a successful CI program – how do we capture the hearts & minds of the employees?

This is really the question at the heart for anyone who has embarked on a CI journey or who is about to embark on one. It is probably in your mind as you've been reading this book. Firstly, I will confess that there is no simple recipe for success—at least not one that I'm aware of. However, this is what I do know: to capture the hearts of minds of employees, the executives need to believe wholeheartedly that what they are undertaking is right for the company both in the short term and long term. This unfortunately is the first problem. Many executives are capricious in the way that they deploy their company strategies. In turn, employees are quite astute at recognizing these attitudes and will not invest in something that they believe has a shelf life of probably 12-18 months at best.

To successfully embed a CI program requires effective change management, particularly for companies that already have an entrenched culture. What I mean by entrenched culture, is that the company has been in existence for a considerable time and operating within a mature industry. This is less of an issue in relatively new companies or companies operating within very immature industries where the pace of growth is rapid. In these companies, employees are probably quite used to change and upheaval so, as a consequence, resistance to any cultural change within such a company would be considerably less of an issue.

Irrespective of whether the company has an already entrenched culture or not, the essential requirement of cultural change is still applicable. If there is no will or motivation to change, then the likelihood of change is minimal at best. The first mistake made in attempting to change a culture is for companies to enforce the change on their workforce. People will only change what they do when it's their decision. This premise is often overlooked or ignored. Real, meaningful change can only occur when people decide to make the change. When change is enforced, this change will only be superficial and can easily be lost. The term 'lip service' if often coined in these situations for good reason; the hearts and minds have not been captured.

I have conducted many process improvement workshops over the many years that I have been undertaking this type of work. One of the key components to a successful process improvement workshop is to ensure that the people in the process are the people coming up with the improvements. The reason for this is that if they *own* the improvement, they have a vested interest in its outcome, and as such will ensure that the change will occur. Too often, facilitators (or process owners via the facilitator) come into a workshop with an idea of what needs to be done and almost enforce this solution on the group. When this occurs, the participants in the workshop quickly realise that the workshop is really just a 'ticking the box' exercise to make the change that management wants. As a result, meaningful acceptance of change will be difficult and unlikely.

From a strategic perspective, people within the company have to be part of the CI journey, not to just implement, but also to be part of the vision. In companies where this has been done well, people from all parts of the business from middle level managers down to the lowest level have been invited into focus groups that are created to work out what the CI vision would look like for the company. This is vital, as it is giving everyone in the company the opportunity to participate and own the vision. This level of acceptance cannot be underestimated as the vision is transferred into a meaningful strategy that can be executed by the people in the company.

Once the CI program has been commenced, constant communication as to the success or challenges of the program is vital to ensure that everyone in the organization is kept up to date. Successful companies have undertaken 'community briefings' where the senior executives responsible for the program go to all parts of the organisation to run

Q&A sessions to ensure that everyone is being heard and that issues are dealt with on a timely basis.

Lastly, accessibility to the program is important if the program is to become part of the DNA of the organization. It is not good enough to have communication advising staff about a great CI program if that is their only exposure. There need to be opportunities for staff who want to be involved, hence the need for CI programs to include not only process improvement but 'hygiene' activities that involve the greater majority of staff.

What is Hoshin Kanri and can it assist a CI program?

Earlier on, I briefly mentioned Hoshin Kanri as a strategic lever in a CI program. Outside of Lean deployments it is a relatively unknown and rarely implemented methodology. Hoshin Kanri, given its name, obviously has its origins firmly rooted in Japan and has been around for a number of years. The name Hoshin Kanri roughly translates to "direction and control" in English. Taking this further, it is really about gaining agreement on which direction to go and then making it happen.

Hoshin Kanri essentially seeks to align actions and outcomes at every level of a company to its overall strategic vision. The aim of this method is to ensure that everyone is pulling in the same strategic direction and that there are no activities occurring that could jeopardize the achievement of the strategic vision.

This strategic planning process is designed to ensure that the corporate strategy, which includes the company vision and goals, are communicated right down to the frontline employees. In turn, each business unit ensures that their strategy is totally aligned to the overall strategy and vision and that all measures and key performance indicators are aligned to the strategy.

The process to create a Hoshin Kanri includes the following objectives:

- Identifying critical business issues facing the organization.

- Establishing business objectives to address these issues.

- Developing supporting strategies.

- Determining goals for each strategy.

- Establishing process performance measures.

- Establishing business fundamental measures.

From what I've discussed to date about successful CI programs, you will note many similarities between some of the objectives stated above and the success factors that I have detailed earlier. Hoshin Kanri is about determining what's important to an organisation, agreeing on what actions need to be undertaken, and then measuring the performance of the company in completing these actions.

To create a Hoshin Kanri environment involves several steps or activities. A number of organisations have adopted a seven-step process to ensure that a systematic method of strategic planning is deployed where progress towards developed strategic goals are effectively managed.

The seven steps:

1. Establish the Organisation's vision.

2. Breakthrough objectives are developed and agreed upon (3-5 year objectives).

3. 12 month objectives are then developed.

4. 12 month objectives are deployed.

5. 12 month objectives are implemented.

6. Ongoing monthly reviews of the progress towards 12 month objectives.

7. Annual review.

This is not a definitive approach and there are many other variations on this method. What I personally like about this approach is that it's a systematic approach from the corporate or organisation's vision down to actionable objectives, which in turn are constantly reviewed to ensure that they are aligned to the organisation's vision.

There is no sugar coating the fact that adopting a Hoshin Kanri approach is not easy and requires total commitment from the CEO down to frontline staff. However, if there is time invested upfront to ensure this approach is adopted, the chances of success for a CI program are greatly enhanced. The reason for this is that a Hoshin Kanri approach ensures that the business and employees are focused on the activities that are aligned to the strategy through a balanced scorecard. Inconsistencies in processes and products will be highlighted, and this in turn will compel business leaders to address these inconsistencies through their CI program.

CI Deployment: A Co-ordinated approach to both project delivery and culture embedding

From observation and experience, CI deployments can follow any of the following strategies:

1. Establishment of an initial centralized Project Management Office (PMO).

2. Establishment of PMO offices in each business unit.

3. Generalized CI culture embedded through the implementation of hygiene behaviours.

4. A combination of a PMO office and a roll-out of a generalized CI culture.

Which strategy should be pursued? I have experienced all four scenarios and whilst there is no 'one size fits all', in reality, some strategies are definitely better than others.

1. Establishment of an initial centralized Project Management Office (PMO)

The biggest mistake that I have seen is the sole creation of a centralized PMO to conduct all CI activities. Whilst this is quite popular with a number of companies and no doubt figures and statistics can be produced to exhort the benefits the company has received as a result of the creation of this central PMO, the longevity of such a program is limited for two reasons.

Firstly, the knowledge and skills are restricted to the PMO office. Consequently business units are not able to fix problems without the engagement with the PMO. Whilst this may create a sense of worth for the PMO, particularly the executive in charge (I have witnessed this for myself), this in time will lead to issues with capacity planning. As such, if the business unit is unable to have their needs addressed they will take the initiative and go to the external market to obtain their own skilled resources.

Secondly, the PMO is mandated with fixing large business-wide issues, not small issues and certainly not creating a prevention strategy. This type of arrangement does not facilitate a change in the culture of the company, just fixing the big problems that are occurring. Quite often, the same problems are brought back to the PMO to be fixed not only by different business units but even the same business unit, following a change in process, restructure etc.

2. Establishment of PMO offices in each business unit

A PMO established in each business unit will at least address the issues that are relative and important to each business unit. However, whilst this is attractive, it also has the same continuing issue of not embedding a consistent culture change across all business units. Furthermore, if there is no central function to coordinate the program, then each business unit is more than likely to go their own way and create differing CI programs and activities which could be at odds to the overarching strategic approach of the company. This was a particular problem that I experienced first-hand at a large financial institution, where the central team had little or no influence over divisional PMOs and, as a result, one business unit decided on a lean program which was at odds to the Lean Six Sigma program that was agreed to at an executive level. This created confusion and significant problems with ongoing training of staff within the organization. Not surprisingly, the strategic approach was eventually abandoned, and business units were left to adopt whatever program that they thought suitable. In time, external resources were just contracted in to 'fix problems'.

3. Generalised CI culture embedded through the implementation of hygiene behaviours.

Embedding a CI culture from the ground up has the advantage of being able to create a culture of CI that is sustainable across the entire organisation. Toyota is a prime ememplar of this strategy. Toyota's approach to CI is presented as a case study in Appendix 2.

The focus of this strategy is on empowering the workforce so that each individual, and not just a select few, has a responsibility for continuous improvement. This creates an environment whereby problems can be solved before they become larger organizational-wide issues—hence why we refer to these 'hygiene behaviours' as a prevention strategy. However, companies need to be well aware that there is at least a 5-year commitment to embedding this type of culture.

A mistake is often made when the term 'ground up' is used to describe embedding a CI program. When this comment is made, what often happens is that a divisional manager or even a general manager institutes their own CI program with the view (read hope) that as the ground swell of training and activities achieves success, the program will be adopted across the rest of the company and embraced at an executive level. I have yet to witness this happening. I have been in a deployment where it has been introduced at a local level and has met resistance from other areas of the company or at an executive level. This resistance was driven by either ego or a strategic perspective or both.

The other aspect of a generalized CI culture is that there must be a component of the program that addresses the substantial process problems that need to be fixed. If there is no component to the program to address this, a number of executives will more than likely think the program is frivolous when there are important issues to be addressed immediately. The saying 'values drives behaviours' is quite relevant when critically analysing these types of deployments. Often there is no immediate benefit in a generalized CI program and immediate benefits are usually a key driver for executives.

4. A combination of a PMO office and a roll-out of a generalized CI culture.

The last strategy is a combination of both a PMO and rollout of a generalized CI culture. This, I believe, is the most successful of the four strategies highlighted. GE successfully adopted a strategy a along similar lines. GE's approach to CI is presented as a case study in Appendix 1.

Both the creation of the PMO and the rollout of the generalized CI culture can occur in tandem. However, if one aspect needs to occur first, then the creation of the PMO office should be the first activity to commence in a CI program. The reason for this is simple. The first decision that needs to be made is what type of methodology will be adopted—that is, whether it is Lean, Six Sigma, Lean Six Sigma or some other hybrid of these methodologies. Once the methodology has been agreed to, the PMO needs to be established and talent recruited with the existing skill sets for the chosen methodology to assist with the implementation of the program and eventual culture change. The PMO should, as a matter of priority, undertake some of the big problems that need to be fixed. This will not only create benefits to justify the initial investment but also promote the success of implementing such a program to the wider audience within the company.

Once the PMO is established and governance is in place, the rollout of the program and the cultural implications need to be planned and carefully managed. This is a not a 12 or 18 month deployment, but a 3-5 year deployment. Therefore, messaging around the program needs to be carefully managed to ensure that unrealistic expectations are not permeating through the company. Key strategic communication as part of a rollout is often overlooked, usually due to senior management thinking that the key messages will be cascaded down through the hierarchical structure of the company. In reality, key program messaging is invariably given lip service at best or, at worst, becomes a casualty of urgent day-to-day issues that need to be addressed. Communication of the program should be targeted and driven from the CEO or at least the head of a division. Messaging should be timely and regular to ensure that employees are under no illusion that the program is important, and will not go away when the next crisis occurs within the division or company as a whole.

In addition, CI training should be provided to all people within the company and not just a select few. However, training should be structured along learning pathways to ensure that as people progress through the company or where talent is shown for CI, additional and more targeted training is provided where needed.

A co-ordinated approach to a centralized PMO and embedding a CI culture truly does provide a level of accelerated benefits that are often not achieved through just a centralised (top-down) approach or a generalised CI cultural (bottom- up) approach. This is due to addressing the immediate needs of using CI to tackle the existing problems within the business, whilst training the workforce to prevent the future problems from becoming an organizational issue.

The graph below illustrates the long term benefits of a adopting the co-ordinated approach (creating an organizational DNA) versus a centralised team. You will note that over time the benefits of a centralised team will tend to flatline in terms of benefit and level of engagement. Levels of engagement suffer because employees will be of the view that fixing the problems is not their concern.

Consequently, the company will struggle to move from a 'fire-fighting' approach for improving products or services to a 'fire prevention' environment.

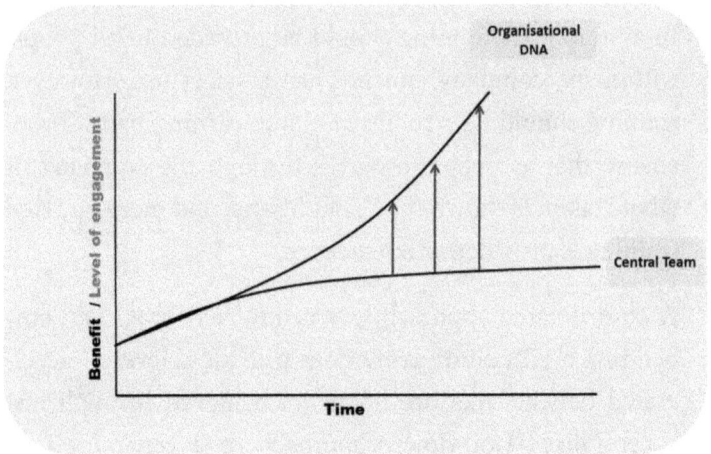

The benefits from an organisation-wide approach become apparent over time.

Program Management of CI

I have discussed at length the key aspects surrounding a successful and not so successful CI program. One aspect that I have not really dealt with to date that is essentially the glue that holds the parts together, is the actual management of the CI program.

What do I mean by program management? The more traditional term is a central office such as Corporate Program Management Office (CPMO), where activities such as projects and resources are coordinated. However, I believe that a true CPMO is more than this: Program management should be responsible for not only the management of projects and resources but also include training, the setting of strategy and the overall management of tactical activities across the business. However, when the CPMO is established there are a number of issues that can often arise that need to be addressed:

The key issue is whether the CPMO is responsible for resourcing CI activities across the business. This can be addressed partly by what type of CI program the business is undertaking. As I discussed earlier, there are four ways in which to roll out a CI program. If the business is seeking to adopt a centralized PMO approach then, traditionally, resourcing will be the responsibility of the CPMO. If, however, the business is looking to decentralize a majority of the CI activities to the various business units, then I strongly suggest that resourcing should be with the business units. I have seen ongoing turf wars being waged where the resourcing is controlled by the CPMO. In these situations, due to resource constraints and business needs not being addressed as a matter of priority, business units will recruit their own professionals to do the work, which can result in centralized resources not being utilized effectively.

Whilst the various business units can be responsible for their own resourcing, it is vitally important that there is some oversight of the resources at the CPMO level. Without this level of oversight of decentralized resourcing, a number of problems can arise:

1. Resources in various business units working on the same problem.

2. Business units adopting variations of the agreed methodology, believing that their unit is unique and therefore requires a different approach or different skilled resources, recruited directly by the business unit.

3. The business units misuse the CI resources by having them engaged in business-as-usual activities that are not directly related to the CI program.

Each or all of these problems are likely to occur without an effective oversight by a CPMO. If these issues are left unchecked, there is a likely chance that these problems can start the demise of an effective CI program.

Let's tackle each of these issues in turn:

1. Resources in various business units working on the same problem.

Where there is no central oversight of the CI program by way of resourcing and activities, problems can arise. At a recent engagement in a large Asian financial institution, I was responsible for coaching a number of green and black belts who were undertaking their initial training project. When I first engaged each of these people, I quickly found that three of these Black Belts were working on an almost identical project involving financial reporting. As each of them was working in a different country within Asia, there was no visibility of what the other areas were doing, so the program manager in each of these areas was focused on the resource tackling the biggest issue in their area, which also happened to be the same issue in other jurisdictions. In tackling the same problem independently of each other, they were wasting resources.

Fortunately, I was able to flag this issue with the centralized office (which, incidentally, was not responsible for resourcing). The office had to work with each of these areas to determine which resource was best placed to continue with the project, whilst the other Black Belts were provided with alternative projects. I have no doubt that this was not an isolated case in that company.

2. Business units adopting variations of the agreed methodology, believing that their unit is unique and therefore requires a different approach or different skilled resources, recruited directly by the business unit.

The second issue where business units adopt variations of the agreed methodology is one that I have witnessed now on at least three occasions. This decision is usually predicated on a misguided belief that their business is unique and requires a different approach from what's being undertaken elsewhere. In addition, this belief is also fueled by the business unit's desire to ensure that their activities are kept 'in-house' and as such, restricting scrutiny from a centralized area. This could be considered a by-product of the silo driven mentalities that often exist in large corporates. Variations in agreed methodology are also created when senior consultants/experts are brought in externally who in turn enforce their own version of the methodology within an area. A strong CPMO is needed is this situation to ensure that oversight is maintained and that outside influences do not create 'variations' that are localized.

Personally, I have no problem with external experts who have been brought in to provide an alternative or improvement to the existing methodology or its implementation. I have done this myself. However, any proposed variations need to be raised with the CPMO, debated and, if there is agreement, deployed across the entire organization.

3. The business units misuse the CI resources by having them engaged in business-as-usual activities that are not directly related to the CI program.

Misusing of CI resources for BAU activities would probably be the most 'cancerous' of the three issues. When I say BAU activities, these are usually dressed up as side projects or short term engagements which drag resources away from what they have been employed to work on. This type of situation is quite insidious. At one deployment, I witnessed one of the best CI project managers in the PMO being lured away to work on a reporting project that was to take only 3 months and this was the way it was sold to the PMO. However, 12 months later the project manager was firmly entrenched in an operational role but desperate to return to the PMO. Another example is where project managers are given 'side projects' which concentrate on BAU activities such as data analysis, reporting templates etc. The attraction being that CI resources due to their training, are inherently valuable to a BU and as such the temptation is to start using these resources for other activities. Whilst I concede the issue of small side projects to benefit a BU is not a problem, it becomes a bit of a slippery slope. Before long, the entire PMO is spending little time working on CI activities and more time on side projects which should be the mandate of the operations team. A strong CPMO and BU PMO together with a detailed CI strategic plan will assist in keeping these types of activities in check.

A simple 4-step approach to rolling out an effective CI program

Having discussed at some length the nature, benefits, implementation strategies and pitfalls of introducing a CI program into an organisation, it is time to bring it all together. In this chapter I describe a simple (not necessarily easy), straightforward process you can follow— one that can be replicated in any business. We should take to heart one of the key facets of process improvement, captured in the adage "simple solutions are often the most effective way to solve process problems." In my view, this maxim applies to both strategic and tactical problems.

There are four key steps that need to be followed to create a successful, positive and lasting CI program. They are:

1. BASELINE: Perform a diagnostic of where the company is currently at, in reference to becoming a CI culture.

2. VISION: Create the CI vision for the company that is in harmony with the strategic vision.

3. UPSKILL: Train and coach the workforce with the necessary skills to create the CI culture.

4. CLOSING THE GAP: Focus on CI activities to realize the vision, and measure CI performance through quarterly and yearly goals.

Notwithstanding the steps that I have highlighted above, this does not in any way diminish the importance of CEO/Executive involvement, communication, and measuring operational performance. These are also important attributes that underpin a successful CI program. However, to ensure that the CI program is set up for success, the four steps highlighted above need to be addressed.

The way to picture these four key steps is quite similar to an ABCDE strategic planning model that I was exposed to a number of years ago. The ABCDE steps are described as: (1) Assessment, (2) Baseline, (3) Components of strategy, (4) Deliver, and (5) Evaluate. In essence, this model is not unduly different to what I'm proposing in terms of creating a successful CI program.

4-step process to develop a CI culture

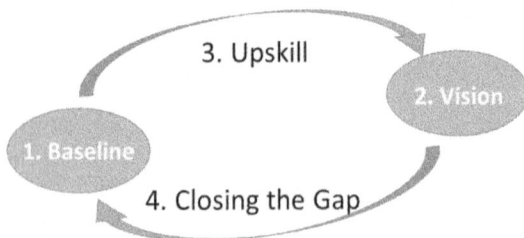

1. Baseline
2. Vision
3. Upskill
4. Closing the Gap

Let's have a closer look at each step in this process:

1. Baseline

This is really about having a deep and impartial view of where your organization is currently in terms of being a CI culture. There are a number of attributes that need to be assessed and scored against agreed criteria. This 'current state' analysis forms the baseline from where we want to lift the organization. I have included a simple check list at the back (see appendix x) which could be used as a starting point to conduct a CI review of the organization.

The impartial view should not be a 'sugar-coated' assessment and is all about baselining the organization. I have witnessed some very 'generous' assessments of a current situation, which do not serve any purpose other than to provide a 'false sense' of the current situation, which in turn creates a diminished need to change the CI culture of the organization.

2. Vision

This is where the organization collectively wants to be. This vision is ideally conducted once study trips have been undertaken to successful CI organisations. This is vitally important, as a successful CI culture needs to be clearly articulated and this can only be achieved through observing successful companies that have achieved this. It would also be advantageous to bring in consultants who have had experience in developing CI cultures to guide the organization in developing its vision.

The CI vision should be an aspirational 5-year goal that covers all aspects of a CI program and how it connects to the organisation's strategic vision.

3. Upskill

As part of the ongoing cultural change that needs to occur in an organization, the upskilling of the workforce is important to ensure that the CI program can be embedded in the organisation's DNA. Whilst it may be advantageous to bring in experienced CI people at the beginning of the journey, it is imperative that the organization upskills its staff. All staff should have exposure to CI training, even if its basic CI hygiene factors such as 5S, basic problem-solving skills, and visual management boards. Management and highly motivated individuals should be provided with more detailed training to ensure that they are suitably equipped to tackle the larger more cross-functional issues that need to be addressed.

Ultimately, basic CI training should be included as part of the induction training for all new staff as is most HR and OH&S training that's usually provided on the first day of work for all new entrants.

4. Closing the Gap

This strategic piece is where the focus and effort is applied towards the activities that will assist in realizing the CI vision that was agreed to at the outset. This might seem obvious; however, I've often seen programs go astray when short term issues hijack a CI initiative. A common example is where organisations have budget pressures such as an uplift in expenses. The CI program is then re-directed to look for 'cost cut' activities. To be successful, the CI program must maintain focus on the end game and resist the culture of 'short termism' that pervades corporate cultures today. I am not advocating that the program should ignore short term goals. However, they should not become the overriding measure of the program.

As 'closing the gap' is about achieving the long term vision, this aspect should involve a number of components such as: (1) ensuring that the trained staff are working on the right activities, (2) long term measures of success linked to the corporate strategy, and (3) milestone events that need to be achieved such as the first 12 months/2years, etc.

Milestone events should ideally incorporate measures such as (i) the number of people trained, (ii) the benefits that have been achieved in terms of extractable dollars, (iii) improved customer interaction measures, and (iv) transformation of key processes.

Regular monthly meetings among executives and monthly communication to the wider company should accompany these activities. The monthly meetings should have a focus on what is and what is not working together with reviews of performance measures. The yearly business planning cycle should incorporate the CI program and do an assessment of the previous year's activities against the plan and recalibrate next year's plan and associated milestones against the strategic plan.

Where to from here?

As businesses continue to evolve through technology-driven disruptions to traditional processes, executives often make comments along the following lines: "What we need is innovation and technology to drive our businesses, not traditional process improvement or continuous improvement." This type of comment, or variations of it, confirms my belief that the need for CI is required more than ever.

In recent years, digitization has been embraced by companies as a way to remove paper and speed up processes. However, in many cases, paper still exists and processes have actually gone backwards in terms of speed and efficiency. The reason for this is that whilst technology has been used to replicate manual processes, no thought has been given as to whether processes were efficient to start with. The result is that automation and digitization puts more pressure on the constraints of the process and creates more inefficiency.

As an analogy, think of a busy 4-lane road that has 3 sets of traffic lights over a 5 kilometre section. If you just increase the width of the road to 6 lanes but keep the traffic lights, all that will happen is that you will create a bigger bottle neck at the traffic lights and no doubt a longer travel time. This is the type of situation that I have been presented with from frustrated process owners following a very expensive rollout of new technology, which has failed to deliver the benefits expected. As technology continues to evolve, the need for CI will continue to be an important toolkit for companies to be as efficient as they can in a competitive environment.

To illustrate the need for technology in 21st century businesses, an excellent article was published by McKinsey in their *McKinsey Quarterly* a couple of years ago. This paper focused on how Amazon has embraced Lean principles in their business. Mark Onetto (at the time, an Amazon Senior Vice President of worldwide operations), who was interviewed by McKinsey for the article, explained what the culture was like at Amazon before Lean. He stated:"Amazon had the belief that most issues could be resolved with technology." Consequently, in the early years there was little emphasis on continuous improvement to resolve any process issues. It should be noted that this was a company that had virtually automated nearly every process in their fulfillment centre. The problem for Amazon and their automated processes was that the fulfillment centre had been designed for books. So, when the decision was made to branch out into other product lines the limitations of the automation was quickly exposed. Another approach was required, one that involved the knowledge and problem-solving skills of the workforce.

Amazon adopted the Lean principle of 'autonomation'[5] which involves keeping automation for low-value, simple work, and using it in a support role for high-value complex tasks. In addition to this concept, Amazon also focused on the enforcement of 'standard work' and Kaizen principles for root-cause analysis to problem solving. As part of this program, everyone in the workforce was exposed to Lean principles with Kaizen teams involving both frontline workers and engineers to solve the everyday problems that were being experienced not only by customers, but also the workforce in meeting the customer needs.

These concepts assisted Amazon to evolve from an on-line bookseller into an electronic commerce and cloud computing company that is now the largest internet-based retailer in the world with a truly global presence.

As we move well into the 21st century, robotics is a term that is becoming more prevalent with the accelerated developments occurring in the world of Artificial Intelligence (AI). I have been at a number of conventions and presentations where I have heard that 'Robotics' is going to revolutionise the business world and replace people in processing centres with robots. Whilst this may be the case, and I have seen some early examples of people being replaced by robotics in payment functions, the fact that cannot be ignored is that there are still business processes to be adhered to. Whether there are people or 'robots' doing the work, the process needs to be efficient in the way it operates. Having a robot do the work incorrectly or inefficiently is not going to be of any benefit to the business.

Conclusion

In closing, I re-emphasise that there is no 'secret' or 'special' way to implement a successful CI program. Success of CI programs to date indicate that the ingredients for a successful program are already in the marketplace. These ingredients have been tried, tested and proven amongst a select group of companies that have managed to achieve a culture based on CI throughout all levels of the organization. Companies that have failed to implement a lasting CI program, and there have been many, have not had all the ingredients or used them at the right time.

I have spent much time exploring why companies have failed to achieve a successful CI program. I have done this because we don't seem to learn the lessons of the past and, as a consequence, the same mistakes continue to be made by companies as they embark on their CI journey. As with any change that is made to the status quo, whether it is changing a habit of a person or the culture of a company, what separates success from failure is usually the will and motivation of the individuals. Therefore, I hope that this book will serve as a guide for companies large or small to understand that CI is not just a methodology or set of business tools to implement through some training and then stand back hoping that it will all just work.

CI is a disciplined approach that requires planning, execution and above all continued focus to ensure that all the elements come together to transform a company into a competitive and nimble organization with a workforce totally energized and valued for what they accomplish.

Appendix 1

Case Study: Six Sigma at General Electric (GE)

Six Sigma made its first appearance at GE around 1995. At the time, the CEO, Jack Welch, had seen the benefits that has been gained at Motorola where the methodology originated. It wasn't the first foray into a CI program by the company. GE had already launched its 'workout' program in the late 1980s. The workout program was similar in structure to 'Lean Kaizen' events where subject matter experts were brought together in a workshop environment to improve a process. Whilst acknowledging that these events were improving the business, Walsh realized that it was not enough to fundamentally change the business, hence his introduction of Six Sigma. It was perceived that this methodology would change the way the company measured performance, in effect, make the organization focus on quality as the key measure of success, which would in turn assist in both driving revenue and reducing costs.

Motorola had focused on the statistical aspects of the methodology to improve product quality. GE saw the methodology as a way of measuring not only product quality but also the quality of inputs and the process itself. It was the initial aim of GE to get to where Motorola was in half the time, but having a relentless focus on quality. In effect, they were looking for Six Sigma to be a 'game changer' for the company.

To make this 'game changer' come to life, the company rolled out Six Sigma in 1996 focusing on three key areas: (1) Leadership, (2) Training, and (3) Project Delivery. It was recognised from the outset that each of these key aspects were critical to the success of program.

Leadership was about ensuring that all leaders in GE were trained and delivered the same message throughout the company. Not only that, Jack Welch ensured that bonuses and promotion within GE were linked directly to the Six Sigma program. Over time, without at least Green Belt training, promotion was not possible. This in itself was a key driver to the success of the program. Welch and his management team not only 'talked the talk' but were highly active and visible as the program was being rolled out. Senior leaders attended training events, conducted Q&A sessions with staff, and made unannounced visits to management Six Sigma review sessions. The aim of these actions was to ensure that there was no ambiguity in the messages that were being delivering from the management board down to the shop floor.

Training was a key component in changing the way that the business operated, and the way employees went about their job. The training was structured to ensure that (1) leadership training focused on data driven decision making, and (2) project-based training (Black and Green belt training) focused on data-based problem analysis. As a result, the business moved away from traditional 'gut-based' or instinctive or experience decision making to a company focused on process data to make key decisions.

Lastly, the success of the program would ultimately be measured through project delivery. That is, the savings and improvements that were made through the completion of process-based projects. A GE phrase that was used widely during this time was 'show me the money', which ensured that all projects delivered real benefits to the company whether it be through cost reduction or revenue uplift. Project delivery also included an established mentoring program where Master Black Belts were actively involved in the process change by assisting Green and Black Belts in making the changes, and by working with stakeholders to ensure the changes were effective.

Given the lengths that the company went to ensure its success, it is easy to see that the company today is still considered a benchmark for the success of Six Sigma methodology. Between 1996 and 1999, GE claimed to have achieved savings in excess of US$4 billion. Since 1999, the savings continue to accrue as the company not only continues to pursue its Six Sigma program, but also Lean via the introduction of a Lean program over the past couple of years as a complimentary CI program.[6]

Appendix 2

Case Study – The Toyota Approach

I described in the introduction how Toyota successfully created the Toyota Production System (TPS) when Japan was rebuilding its manufacturing base after World War 2. The TPS system still exists today and stands as a testament to a successful CI culture that has been created and sustained for well over 60 years.

The Toyota approach is built on two fundamental core concepts: (1) The foundation is the *Toyota Way* which describes the values of the company, and (2) the *Toyota Business Practices (TBP)*, which describes in detail how the employees within Toyota go about realising and implementing the Toyota Way.

1. Toyota Way

The Toyota Way which is described as the values of the company, is broken down into two pillars: (1) Continuous Improvement, and (2) Respect for People. Toyota from the outset has avoided gimicky concepts and catch phrases. Instead, it has created a philosophy which transcends different languages and cultures. Toyota is clear when communicating the need for the 'Toyota Way'. The company states: "we are never satisfied with where we are and always improve our business by putting forth your best ideas and effort. We respect people, and believe the success of our business is created by individual efforts and good teamwork"[7].

Let's look at each component of the Toyota Way[7].

Continuous Improvement is the foundation of the TPS and involves three principles (i) Challenge, (ii) Kaizen, and (iii) Genchi Genbutsu. Challenge is simply meeting the challenges of achieving the long-term vision with courage and creativity. Kaizen is the approach that Toyota takes in continuously improving business operations with the focus being on innovation and evolution.

It is important to note here that Toyota's use of the word 'Kaizen' is different to the way the term is used in companies today. In a lot of businesses, the use of the term 'Kaizen' relates to workshops where processes are analysed by people in the process over a short period of time (1-2 days). Processes are mapped and simple solutions are generated to improve the process. Whilst this may happen in Toyota, the term 'Kaizen' is used to describe the philosophy used at Toyota. This philosophy is based on three core tenements:

- Kaizen Mind and Innovative Thinking

- Building Lean Systems and Structure

- Promoting Organisational Learning

Genchi Genbutsu, the last principle of Continuous Improvement, is a Japanese term which loosely translates to 'go to the source'. This is about creating the behaviour amongst the staff to always go to the source to find the facts and make the correct decision. This is achieved through effective and collaborative consensus building.

'Respect for People' is the second component and is about respecting others within the organisation and making every effort to understand each other. This includes respect for the stakeholders, mutual trust and responsibility, and sincere communication. In addition, there is a focus on teamwork where sharing the opportunities of development are encouraged so that the individual and team performance can be maximised.

2. Toyota Business Practices

Toyota states in its communication to its employees: Toyota Business Practices can be described as "systematic patterns of work processes that integrate the wisdom of all employees in the pursuit of continual growth and satisfaction."

In essence, Toyota Business Practices follows Deming's PDCA approach of Lean thinking. It is an 8-step approach to problem solving. The process focusses on clarifying the problem being experienced and then analysing for root cause. Once this has been determined, the counter-measures (solutions) are developed and implemented. If successful, the countermeasures are standardized into the process in order to minimise the risk of the problem reoc-curring. The simple 8-step process is as follows:

1. Clarify the Problem

2. Break down the Problem

3. Set a Target (improvement target)

4. Analyse the Root Cause

5. Develop the Countermeasures

6. See the Countermeasures through

7. Evaluate both Results and Processes

8. Standardize Successful Processes.

Toyota Business Practices

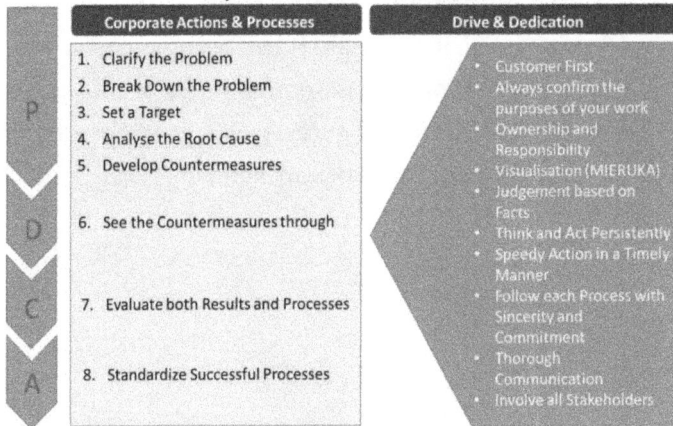

Corporate Actions & Processes	Drive & Dedication
1. Clarify the Problem 2. Break Down the Problem 3. Set a Target 4. Analyse the Root Cause 5. Develop Countermeasures	• Customer First • Always confirm the purposes of your work • Ownership and Responsibility • Visualisation (MIERUKA) • Judgement based on Facts
6. See the Countermeasures through	• Think and Act Persistently • Speedy Action in a Timely Manner
7. Evaluate both Results and Processes	• Follow each Process with Sincerity and Commitment
8. Standardize Successful Processes	• Thorough Communication • Involve all Stakeholders

What I like about the Toyota approach is that for every action there is an underlying driver — why it is important to the employee, the company and ultimately the customer. They list a number of drivers such as "Customer First", "Ownership and Responsibility", and "Thorough Communication", among others.

If you are familiar with the PDCA Lean methodology, you will see the similarities in this approach. This is the fundamental philosophy of Lean. Toyota lives this approach throughout the entire company.

Even today, if you have the opportunity to do a site visit to a Toyota production facility, which they readily provide, you can see both the Toyota Way and Toyota Business Practices in action. From the way employees approach their role on the production line to the Visual Management boards that are located throughout the site, the company and the employees live these principles. This to me is the best example of a CI program that I've seen. It has become part of the DNA of a corporation and no doubt, it has been a main driver in Toyota's continued success since its early origins as a car manufacturer over 70 years ago.

Appendix 3

CI Maturity Assessment Example

	Level 1 Non-existent	Level 2 Ad-hoc	Level 3 Managed	Level 4 Optimising	Level 5 World Class
Process Architecture	Process architecture not defined with limited or no documentation available. No overarching standard agreed upon	Not in common use across organisation, however, there has been some effort to implement architecture.	It is a key management tool as part of both operational management and strategic planning. It is used to support decision making	It is used regularly across the organisation by both executives and managers. Architecture modelling is being utilised.	It is accepted as part of the decision making process. All information and artefacts are maintained centrally together with modelling based tools
CI & Process measurement	Few measures are in use but only localised and ad-hoc for local reporting purposes	Some processes are measured but performance evaluation is independent of process and usually for compliance purposes	Measuring is standard practice and is used and reported widely. The CI program has organisation wide measures and all top level processes have measures in place	Measuring is occurring at every level of the organisation to assess and improve processes. Measurement control is embedded in the organisation's culture.	CI Decisions are made on process and CI performance. All measurement is systematic, accurate and continuous. All problems are evaluated with corresponding measures
Strategic Planning	All CI activities are localised with no strategic view and no strategic planning	Some areas have a CI program in place but is not consistent across the organisation.	There is an overarching strategic plan and purpose for the CI program.	The CI strategic plan is a 5 year plan with yearly milestones in place to assess progress.	Strategic planning of CI activities is part of the organisation's overall business strategic planning process and is regularly reported on to key stakeholders and employees.
CI knowledge	Limited or no knowledge of basic CI principles across the workforce	Some areas of the business have basic CI knowledge and/or people trained in CI	The workforce in general have been provided with basic CI training with a number of people considered as expert in CI	All workforce trained with a select number of people having a high degree of expertise in CI. Considered mandatory as part of operational training	All employees trained and with Managers having CI experience. CI training is part of the Learning pathways and CI knowledge/ qualifications considered mandatory for promotion.
CI Hygiene behaviours	No Visual Management or basic CI behaviours evident (such as 5S and problem solving tools using PDCA)	Limited use of Visual Management Boards and tools such as 5S and PDCA	Visual Management Boards/5S and problem solving is evident throughout the business.. However, the behaviours are not standardised	CI Hygiene is wholly adopted and standardised across the business with best practice sharing.	All business decisions and problem solving is based on metrics used on visual management boards. Problem solving at a team level solves 80% of all business issues without the need to go outside the team for assistance.
Program Governance	No governance in place.	Some governance evident but very localised and within business units only. No strategic view of activities	Basic strategic overview of CI activities. However,, there is still evidence of duplicated activities and between business units and standardisation is still an issue	Full governance or all CI activities in place both at a local level and at a strategic level. Both basic CI and transformation activities have proper governance and oversight	Governance of CI activities are in line with the 3-5 strategic plan. Level of governance is in line with the type of CI activities in place. Resources full utilised and no duplication of activities.

Notes

1 Nadia Bhuiyan, Amit Baghel, (2005) "An overview of continuous improvement: from the past to the present", Management Decision, Vol. 43 Issue: 5, pp.761-771, https://doi.org/10.1108/00251740510597761

2 Philip Atkinson (2010) "'Lean' is a Cultural Issue", Management Services, Summer 2010, pp.35-41, http://www.lean-six-sigma-od-training.com/uploads/7/1/5/0/7150143/lean-change-philipatkinson.pdf

3 Association for Information and Image Management (AIIM), http://www.aiim.org/What-is-BPM-Business-Process-Management#sthash.IWo6kUhR.dpuf

4 See Imre Hegedus (2008), *Business Process Management: Insights and Practices for Sustained Transformation*, Ark Group

5 *Autonomation* ("intelligent automation") is a feature of machine design to effect the principle of *jidoka* used in the Toyota Production System (TPS) and Lean manufacturing. Jidoka is one of the two pillars of the Toyota Production System along with just-in-time. Jidoka highlights the causes of problems because work stops immediately when a problem first occurs. This leads to

improvements in the processes that build in quality by eliminating the root causes of defects (https://www.lean.org/lexicon/jidoka).

6 "The skinny on Lean: Use it of lose it—GE appliances and the Lean Process, http://pressroom.geappliances.com/facts/the-skinny-on-lean-230762

7 The Toyota Way 2001, 2nd edition (Jan 2002), Toyota Motor Corporation

About the Author

Gregory (Greg) Kilbey is an independent consultant of Lean Six Sigma in both Process and Continuous Improvement. Greg is based in Melbourne, Australia and works extensively throughout Australia and South East Asia for a range of clients from multi-national corporations through to health agencies in Australia.

Greg holds a Bachelor of Science degree in Applied Mathematics and Statistics from Monash University as well as a Masters Degree in Accounting from the University of Southern Queensland.

In addition, to his consultancy work, Greg also trains employees in Process and Continuous Improvement as well as lecturing in Business Process Management and Business Information Systems at Swinburne University of Technology.

Greg has spoken on Lean Six Sigma and Deployment of Continuous Improvement at various conferences in Australia and been published in various journals.